Breaking the Power of Corruption

I0202502

By Bob Mumford

LIFECHANGERS®

P.O. Box 3709 ❖ Cookeville, TN 38502
931.520.3730 ❖ lc@lifechangers.org

PLUMBLINE

Published by:

LIFECHANGERS ®
LIBRARY SERIES

P.O. Box 3709 | Cookeville, TN 38502
(800) 521-5676 | www.lifechangers.org

All Rights Reserved
ISBN 978-1-940054-10-0

Breaking the Power
of Corruption

Contents

Introduction

Peace be to the brethren, and love [Agape] with faith, from God the Father and the Lord Jesus Christ. Grace be with all those who love our Lord Jesus Christ with incorruptible love (Eph. 6:23–24).

Paul takes us through spiritual warfare and teaches us about the full armor of God throughout the book of Ephesians and ends his writing with a blessing of incorruptibility. Paul is saying that it is possible to live without corruption and to love Jesus with an incorruptible love. The word corruption (Strongs #861) is used seven times in the New Testament. When I first began to understand this I called it "Unshared Love." Timothy called it immortality, which in Greek is "incorruption" (see 2 Tim. 1:10). It is a shame that the word was translated immortality leading us to think that we don't die. Living without corruption is the freedom for which Christ set us free!

We have been dealing with corruption since Eve gave Adam a bite of an apple. Genesis 6:12 says, "All flesh was corrupted." Because of corruption God flooded the entire planet, sparing only Noah and his family because they did not yield to corruption and found favor in God's eyes. The waters of Noah play an important role in displacing corruption.

The Old Testament states that corruption is a defect (see Lev. 22:25; Deut. 32:5). We will look at the theme of corruption throughout Scripture; see the connection to temptation and lying against the truth; as well as how baptism and the Cross break the power of corruption.

Presuppositions

I met with a group of 20 leaders one time when the Lord gently said to me, "Ask them what their presuppositions are." I assumed that these 20 leaders were all at the same spiritual and theological place I was. Was that a shock! When I started asking about their presuppositions, there must have been 30 different ones—everyone had their own and some had a couple new ones I'd never heard of. It was such a revelation that everyone was speechless. So, I want to begin by establishing four presuppositions about corruption so that we can all be on the same page.

Presupposition #1. Corruption happened before the beginning of creation. "For the creation (nature) was subjected to frailty (to futility, condemned to frustration), not because of some intentional fault on its part, but by the will of Him Who so subjected it" (Rom. 8:20 AMP). It wasn't an accident. Father subjected creation to futility because He wanted to bring the entire creation to its redemptive purpose. Thus, we are made aware of the *inevitability* of the Incarnation. Our help had to come from the outside—from Father Himself—because every human being is ungoverned. Paul explained the entrance of corruption: "Just as through one man sin entered into the world, and death through sin, and so death spread to all men, because all sinned" (Rom. 5:12).

I recently read a book[1] that told a story about three fisherman on a very primitive island that had no cultural influence. The three men were in a boat, and they all caught fish. One caught the biggest fish of anyone that day and noticed the other two staring at the fish in an odd way. He suddenly became aware of what he called "the evil eye"—envy. He didn't want them to look at him with envy, so he immediately cut the fish into three parts, giving each of them an equal part of his large fish.

The "evil eye" is an everyday occurrence—it is pervasive and ubiquitous. When someone pulls up in their new Mercedes, we feel a surge inside us of something that can only be identified as corruption. We don't mind if the president of a company drives a Mercedes, but we certainly don't want our neighbor to have one when we're driving a Ford. Corruption emerges very subtly and has been around since the Garden of Eden.

Presupposition #2. Grace is more than unmerited favor. Grace is a bestowal of value upon a person even when they are not virtuous. Father bestowed on us value through the New Birth. Paul categorized all human beings as having lost their governing factor. In order to get us out of that predicament, God had to send us a Person Who was governed. All that is

[1]Schoeck, Helmut (1987). *Envy: A Theory of Social Behavior* ISBN-13: 978-0865970649 Harcort, Brace

humanly created must be regenerated, transformed, and/or instructed—that is why there is a new creation. God bestowed value on us by imparting the Seed of *Agape* to us through Christ. When we receive that value and respond to it, it leads to a change in our behavior and that leads to freedom. We are released from corruption including obsessive compulsive disorders.

It is our responsibility to properly respond to the *Agape* that was imparted to us. This means that *Agape* changes our behavior so that we produce fruit 30, 60, or 100-fold as discussed in Matthew 13:8 and that coruption is dimishing in us. Either my desires are governed, not governed, or somewhere in between. We will look more closely at the process of maturing from being 30% governed to 60% governed and reaching the goal of being 100% governed by Father God and His Kingdom. 2 Peter 1:4 states, "For by these He has granted to us His precious and magnificent promises, so that by them you may become partakers of the divine nature, having escaped the corruption that is in the world by lust." That promise is the very backbone of this entire *Plumbline*.

Presupposition #3. No law can change our desires. The Hebrews did things a certain way with more than 400 laws to further define the 10 Commandments, but when Jesus came, He did everything completely different—this is interpolation or what I call the Hebrew correction. Jesus is reaching through the law for our hearts because He knew that no law can change our desires. If an ungoverned person wants something bad enough, they'll change or reinterpret as many Bible verses as needed to make sure they get it. That's interpolation. The basic thing that governs most people is their desires. "For the Law never made anything perfect—but instead a better hope is introduced through which we [now] come close to God" (Heb. 7:19 AMP).

My wife, Judith, and I were remodeling a house in the 1970s, and we had a table built that cost more than $600 and had about 50 coats of polymer on it. When it was all finished I put the level on the table and there was a big hollow space under the level. The table was corrupted. It was completely warped. When the contractor said we had to take the whole table apart and start over, I reacted and said, "We're not taking the table apart, we're just going to bend the level!" Instead of going through all the work of

making the corrupted table right, I wanted to change the standard. Changing the standard to accommodate our corruption is very prevalent today.

These three presuppositions offer us a literal fulfillment of the promise of Christ Who said, "And you will know the truth, and the truth will make you free" (John 8:32). Our goal is personal behavioral freedom from corruption.

Before we look at our subject in Scripture, let's define corruption in today's language.

Understanding Corruption

> [22]*Professing to be wise, they became fools,* [23]*and exchanged the glory of the incorruptible God for an image in the form of corruptible man and of birds and four-footed animals and crawling creatures (Rom. 1:22–23).*

Merriam Webster defines corruption as:

Dishonest or illegal behavior especially by powerful people (such as government officials or police officers); the act of corrupting someone or something; something that has been changed from its original form; impairment of integrity, virtue, or moral principle (depravity); decay or composition; inducement to wrong by improper or unlawful means (as bribery); a departure from the original or from what is pure or correct; archaic: an agency or influence that corrupts.

A friend of mine was telling me about his experience as a young man of having a prominent Bible teacher stay with his family. He thought it was going to be really neat. The young man was very impressed as he watched the Bible teacher spend three hours every morning reading Scripture and studying. Then he watched the way that he related to his wife and realized that he was the prickliest curmudgeon you'd ever want to come across. He was irritable, harsh, short-tempered, and could crush you in a word because his coffee wasn't hot or was given to him a minute later than he expected. The young man didn't know what the answer was, but if three hours in the Scripture every day produced that, he didn't want any part of it! He wanted to please the Father but realized that if you didn't couple it with dealing with corruption and your own desires, you had competing interests. Corruption is like having a monkey on your back—you have deep, uncontrollable desires that you can't get rid of. Unless you turn, face the thing, and set it aside, you cannot be single minded in your pursuit of pleasing God.

Corruption is the first cause; it functions in society as the default. In other words, when our volitional and intentional goals are frustrated or delayed, we return for answers and comfort to the first cause and determining factor. Corruption functions as the default value system in our society in the following ways.

- Drugs, alcohol, and sex/pornography
- Control, anger and/or manipulation
- Deception, false promises, and hidden agendas
- Greed in its unmitigated and myriad of forms
- Envy and the evil eye

Corruption creates the appearance of being *volitional*, but it actually functions and increases both overtly and covertly through agendas until it becomes the ultimate value system. Corruption can and does increase until it threatens the literal survival of our entire civilization.[2]

My son, Eric, in his writings in the *God Magnified* series explains corruption as *eros* the counterfeit of *Agape*:

> The counterfeit of *Agape* is *eros*—self-love —individualism manifested in self-indulgence, self-will, and self-worth-ship. In the Scriptures, *eros* is called "corruption" and "iniquity, transgression, and sin" (Ex. 34:7) because it effectively *displaces* self-sharing. If God was a solitary Being and "God is love," God would have to be Self-love (*eros*), but God is an "Us" in Oneness—God is Triune-*Agape*. The eternal purpose of these three, sacrificial Self-sharers is that you and I "may become partakers [*sharers*] of the divine nature [*e.g. Agape*] having escaped the corruption [*de-gene-ration in eros– individualism*] that is in the world by lust [*desiring desire itself for self*]" (1 Pet. 1:4).
>
> Before creation, however, the three Self-sharers knew mankind would fall and purposed to come to us in a new, incorruptible, Self-sharing Man. The Apostle John testified, "No one has seen God [*Triune-Spirit*] at any time; the only begotten God [*uncreated Son "made*

[2]For more information on this topic, read *Collapse: How Societies Choose to Fail or Succeed* by Jared Diamond, published by Penguin Books.

flesh"] Who is in the bosom of the Father, **He has explained Him** [*spiritual Reality*]" (John 1:18). What humanity as individualists "could not do weak as it was through the flesh, God did: **sending** His own Son in the likeness of sinful flesh and as an offering for sin, He condemned sin [*corruption, self-worth-ship*] in the flesh" (Rom. 8:3).

Minds in Corruption

I fear, lest somehow, as the serpent deceived Eve by his craftiness, so your minds may be corrupted from the simplicity that is in Christ. (2 Cor. 11:3).

To further understand the depth of corruption and its source, I turn to T. Austin Sparks who has been my spiritual mentor for many years. His insight into the soul is noteworthy.

Deception is not something out there that is put upon us willy-nilly, or in spite of ourselves. All deception has its own ground in man. What is that ground? It is the fact that man is now a psychical being. Now if you can get to the bottom of that, if you can apprehend that, you will understand the whole thing. The ground of all this is in the fact that man is a psychical being, and when Satan interfered with man at the beginning and man consented along the line of his own soul-life, Satan made man suitable to his own government. It was not that he came and set himself up as man's ruler and subjected man by sheer force to his own government. How did he do it? By breaking into that realm in man's being where man was linked with God, and that was in the realm of man's spirit. "He that is joined to the Lord is one spirit," and man was in fellowship and communion with God by means of his spirit, not his soul, not his body. These two were under the government of his spirit. The enemy, the Deceiver came to man's soul, and instead of man reacting by his spirit-fellowship with, and knowledge of, God, he dropped down on to his soul, came out of his spirit and reacted in his soul.

What is soul? It is reason, emotion, feeling, desire, and then, of course, choice, or will. And the enemy reasoned through the desires and captured the will by deception. You see what happened when man violated the very organ of his union with God, his spirit.... So the enemy governs man, and the whole of the race now through the nature of the soul-life. What is the basis of deception? It is just that! How do you get a counterfeit Holy Ghost operating? By reason of your psychical nature. You can become mediumistic in your very psychical nature and open all the avenues of your being to supernatural guidance and come under the power, the sway, dominion, of deceiving spir-

its operating in a multitude of ways. You can so suspend your soul and come into a state of utter passivity that you are open to everything to play upon you. You can have your quiet hour in your soul, which is the most perilous hour of your life. That happens by suspending all spiritual activity and becoming utterly passive and opening your psychical being, which is a most dangerous thing. God never asks you to become spiritually passive. Waiting upon God is not being spiritually passive. God wants us active in spirit even when waiting on Him in silence.[3]

And the Earth was Corrupt

[11] The earth was depraved and putrid in God's sight, and the land was filled with violence (desecration, infringement, outrage, assault, and lust for power). [12] And God looked upon the world and saw how degenerate, debased, and vicious it was, for all humanity had corrupted their way upon the earth and lost their true direction (Gen. 6:11–12).

Within the Old and New Testaments there are 80 uses of the word "corrupt" and "corruption." Even back in Genesis the earth was corrupt and violence was common. Not much has changed since then.

---

[3]T. Austin Sparks (n.d.). *Christ the Power of God*. Chapter 3, Aug 8: Minds in Corruption. Retrieved from http://www.austin-sparks.net/english/openwindows/003309.html

In the first nine months of 2015, there were more than 290 mass shootings in America. The corruption that Father saw in Genesis required drowning the whole world except for the remnant of Noah and his family. God then put a rainbow in the sky as a promise that He would never do that again (see Gen. 9:12-15). And God doesn't change—He is the same yesterday, today, and forever (see Heb. 13:8). Today He looks down and sees our corruption and knows that it, too, must be drowned. Just as in the days of Noah, when corruption becomes overly demanding or culturally prevalent, Father intervenes. This is the phenenomon called divine intervention. When we are buried in water and brought up we are set free from corruption. But this time He's drowning us one at a time *out* of corruption and the old creation and into a new Kingdom lifestyle (see Matt. 16:16). Our old way of being governed is held under water so that the new government of God can emerge. When we move out of the old creation and into the new Kingdom (see Col 1:13), we are governed differently.

Our corruption rears its ugly head from generation to generation no matter how we may try to camouflage it. Consider Jotham who while reigning 16 years in Jerusalem was recorded as doing right in the sight of the Lord according to all that Uziah had done. During his reign the people continued to act corruptly. Nehemiah, the prophet, said, "We have acted very corruptly against You …" (Neh. 1:7).

Paul spoke of the corruption present in him in Romans 7:19-20 (AMP):

For I fail to practice the good deeds I desire to do, but the evil deeds that I do not desire to do are what I am [ever] doing. Now if I do what I do not desire to do, it is no longer I doing it [it is not myself that acts], but the sin [principle] which dwells within me fixed and operating in my soul].

Corruption is a spontaneous and unexpected phenomenon. It appears when we're least expecting it.

Corruption in Scripture

As I mentioned, there are more than 80 uses of the word "corrupt" in Scripture. Following are a few of the more significant uses. I've included a complete list in the Appendix. In Scripture, the words for corruption refer to physical degeneration or decay (see Is. 52:14; Lev. 22:25; Dan. 10:8). The New Testament also adds decomposing of the material world and of nature (see Acts 7:27, 31; 13:34-37; 1 Cor. 15:42, 50; Rom. 8:21, Col 2:22; 2 Pet. 2:12). But Peter and Paul take it a step further to mean religious and moral corruption (see 2 Pet 1:4; 2:19; Gal. 6:8). Let's look at some specific references to corruption in Scripture.

- Genesis 6:11-12. "¹¹Now the earth was *corrupt* in the sight of God, and the earth was filled with violence. [12]And God looked on the earth, and behold, it was *corrupt*; for all flesh had *corrupted* their way upon the earth." Note that the word "corrupt" is used three times in this one verse. After God said this, He drowned the whole world. As we mentioned earlier, corruption requires the waters of Noah (see Gen. 9:13-17).

- Daniel 6:3-5: "[3]Then this Daniel began distinguishing himself among the commissioners and satraps because he possessed an extraordinary spirit, and the king planned to appoint him over the entire kingdom. [4]Then the commissioners and satraps began trying to find a ground of accusation against Daniel in regard to government affairs; but they [governmental officials] could find no ground of accusation or *evidence of corruption*, inasmuch as he was faithful, and no negligence or corruption was to be found in him. [5]Then these men said, 'We shall not find any ground of accusation against this Daniel unless we find it against him with regard to the law of his God.'" I love the story of Daniel. Even as a youth he was without blemish and wise and because no corruption was found in him, he was recruited to serve in the king's palace. For three years he was fed the king's food and taught the ways of the Chaldeans. "But Daniel determined in his heart that he would not defile himself by [eating his portion of] the king's rich and dainty food or by [drinking] the wine which he drank; therefore he requested of the chief of the eunuchs that he might [be allowed] not to defile himself" (Dan 1:8). He was surrounded by a corrupt nation, yet he refused to let anything defile him. The Chaldean government could not find any evidence of corruption in Daniel! I look at my own life and ask myself, "Would they find any corruption in me?"

- Nehemiah 1:7-8, "We have acted very corruptly against You and have not kept the commandments, statutes, and ordinances which You commanded Your servant Moses." The ordinances Father gave them were designed so that Israel would live by the Kingdom value system of bearing the fruit of *Agape* and act differently than all the other nations. Their corruption was the failure to respond to that Kingdom value system.

- Mark 11:17, "My house shall be called a house of prayer for all the nations, but you have made it a robbers' den." This had nothing to do with buying and selling in the church. Jesus was saying that ungoverned desire had captured Father's house. Corruption in the form of ungoverned desire has captured Father's house all over the globe. And denominational, ungoverned desire is just as bad as sinful, ungoverned desire. The system is full of private doctrines, private kingdoms, and private motives all in the name of religion. Jesus rebuked the Pharisees for taking the widow's houses in the name of religion and using Scripture to do it (see Matt. 23:14). Ungoverned desire will even use

Scripture to get what it wants. When you make external laws, *eros* is so clever that it is able to use the laws for its own corrupt purposes. Unless we move from external to internal, we'll never be able to get free! John Oman, a reformed author says, "If it was not for divine intervention, the Church would be the most corrupt institution in the earth."[4]

- Romans 7:16-19: "[17]So now, no longer am I the one doing it, but sin which indwells me. [18]For I know that nothing good dwells in me, that is, in my flesh; for the wishing is present in me, but the doing of the good is not. [19]For the good that I wish, I do not do; but I practice the very evil that I do not wish." Romans sheds an interesting light on how spontaneous and unexpected corruption can be. Suppose you are sitting in church when the offering plate comes by and there is a new $50 bill on the top of the pile. Suddenly corruptions says, "This is Lord's provision for you." You weren't thinking that before—it just manifests in you. It is a form of slavery because we become captured by it. It's not something we premeditate, but instead of recognizing what it is and dismissing it, we automatically act on it and that is what costs us!

- Galatians 6:8, "For the one who sows to his own flesh will from the flesh reap corruption, but the one who sows to the Spirit will from the Spirit reap eternal life." This enables us to see that what

[4]John Oman (1923). *Vision & Authority*. Houghter and Stoughton.

we sow produces good fruit or corrupt fruit. What is being manifested externally is the nature of what is being manifested in our person. If we sow corruption, we will certainly reap the same.

- Ephesians 6:23-24: "²³Peace be to the brethren, and love [*Agape*] with faith, from God the Father and the Lord Jesus Christ. ²⁴Grace be with all those who love our Lord Jesus Christ with a love *incorruptible.*" When someone says they love Jesus with an incorruptible love, it has to do with intention; it doesn't mean they do it right all the time. What God asks of us is that we love Him with all our heart, soul, mind, and strength and He'll take care of the rest.

- Romans 12:9, "Let love be without hypocrisy. Abhor what is evil; cling to what is good." The implication here, as we mentioned previously, is that we can fake *Agape*. Just think about a time when you greeted someone and told them you had been praying for them when that never entered your mind. Just like God flooded the earth to destroy corruption in the Old Testament, the Temple in the New Testament had to be destroyed because it represented ungoverned desire.

- James 3:14: "But if you have bitter jealousy and selfish ambition in your heart, do not be arrogant and so lie against the truth." Why would we lie against the truth? Because of ungoverned desire. Not only have we lied against the truth, but we have lied to ourselves. Our conscience says, "You shouldn't eat that second piece of cake" and immediately we begin maneuvering and reasoning until we can justify eating what we want. Then we go through all the pain and crazies of a guilty conscience because our desire ruled us. This can be sexual, financial, emotional—name any desire that is ungoverned, they are all corrupt.

- 2 Peter 1:4, "For by these He has granted to us His precious and magnificent promises, so that by them you may become partakers of the divine nature, having escaped the corruption that is in the world by lust." Escaping corruption suggests that we are walking in the freedom that Christ promises us in John 8:32 when He said, "You will know the truth, and the truth will make you free."

- 2 Peter 2:19, "Promising them freedom while they themselves are slaves of corruption; for by what a man is overcome, by this he is enslaved." A lot of cowboy movies have a corrupt preacher in them. He usually quotes Scripture and kills people. The movie producers were capitalizing on the fact that quoting Scripture doesn't automatically produce positive behavior. However, when we have escaped corruption, we can walk in the freedom that the Kingdom promises.

The word corruption is used throughout the Old and New Testaments. You can't bribe the postmodern with heaven or bribe them with hell because they really don't care about either. They don't believe it because they don't see any difference in the lives of those who were bribed or blackmailed. But they understand being governed by something. So when our desire is to go to an X-rated movie but we don't go because someone may see us, that is not Kingdom— that is being ruled by fear. Like other post-moderns, we want there to be a connection between what we believe and what we do.

The Phenomenon of Corruption

If corruption is *the* central issue of the human dilemma and Scripture seems to point to this as the ignored, unsolvable, and misunderstood quandary, such insight would cause us to see the Kingdom more perfectly, supplying a comprehensive grasp of the governmental description of the meta-narrative that seeks to illumine the heart of the Father to His Own creation. This causes me to ask one simple question: Father, what are You most concerned about?

All sin is *volitional*. We inherited our corruption through no fault of our own (see Rom. 5:12). What *is* volitional is our choice to sow to the spirit or sow to the flesh; this is where we reap the fruit of *Agape* or the fruit of corruption. Corruption has been woven into the fabric of the human mind, emotions, and will with such intricacy that it triggers deceit, releasing it to function in some autonomic manner. This is what Paul meant when he said, "So now, no longer am I the one doing it, but sin which dwells in me" (Rom. 7:17).

It is most important that we do not dismiss this biblical insight and begin blaming the devil or unintentionally assign what Paul is saying as an excuse or some other form of avoidance of human responsibility. As we have learned in times past, corruption causes us to run, hide, and shift blame. A pastor had the impulse to pat a woman in his congregation on the behind. Without thinking, he gave in to the autonomic reaction, causing himself all kinds of problems. That experience caused him to grow up in a number of ways! That which is autonomic, like breathing, should arouse our concern because without freedom from corruption it is very difficult to mature in *Agape*.

The phenomenon of corruption can be understood something like this:

A. Corruption is contagious. The reasons corruption seem to increase in velocity and speed is because corruption is contagious. Once corruption is released in the earth, it gathers speed and momentum. "Do not be so deceived and misled! Evil companionships (communion, associations) corrupt and deprave good manners and morals and character" (1 Cor. 15:33 AMP).

B. As corruption increases, so does volitional sin because it engages our human will/emotions to go our own way and do our own thing.

Although we inherited corruption, we are responsible not to yield to it or give ourselves to it but to live by the Kingdom value system.

C. Corruption is the primary pollution from which the entire creation must be set free. It is Father's most serious concern. His goal is "that the creation itself also will be set free from its slavery to corruption into the freedom of the glory of the children of God" (Rom. 8:21).

D. Corruption manifests in systems or authority structures such as natural family, culture and tradition, political entities, economic entities, and religious entities. Each system has been so corrupted that it requires them all, without exception, to be corrected or annulled for the purpose of Father becoming all in all (see 1 Cor. 15:28). Paul makes this annulment very evident in 1 Corinthians 15:24, "After that comes the end (the completion), when He delivers over the kingdom to God the Father after rendering inoperative and abolishing every [other] rule and every authority and power" (AMP).

E. It is entirely possible that biblical idea of volitional *action* and non-volitional *corruption* could explain the latest insights into the subliminal, revealing the unconscious or subconscious mind functioning in ways that are not ordinarily known or accepted. We can see this in Paul's description of man's captivity: "So now, no longer am I the one doing it, but sin which dwells in me" (Rom. 7:17). Leonard Mlodinow in his latest book, *Subliminal: How Your Unconscious Mind Rules Your Behavior* reinforces the idea of "the two-tiered brain." It may be that corruption itself is what produced such a phenomenon.

Five Aspects of the Kingdom

No longer do I call you slaves, for the slave does not know what his master is doing; but I have called you friends, for all things that I have heard from My Father I have made known to you (John 15:15).

And the Scripture was fulfilled which says, "AND ABRAHAM BELIEVED GOD, AND IT WAS RECKONED TO HIM AS RIGHTEOUSNESS," and he was called the friend of God (James 2:23).

Our journey, typified by Israel's wilderness journey from Egypt to the Land of Promises, becomes an existential necessity because it provides the life-labs and living opportunity for us to exercise the *Agape* we were inseminated at the New Birth. *Agape* is the metaphysical energy of the Kingdom of God that has come to earth! The concept of intimacy stated as Father's Own desire (John 14:21-23) can be explained in five observations. Each of these five have, as their prerequisite, the understanding of what it means to have identified and yielded the deepest part of one's being—our personal sovereignty.

1. It is the nature of the Kingdom journey to precipitate insemination and cultivation of *Agape* until our capacity to love God and love our neighbor (fusion) begins to mature and bear fruit 30%, 60%, and eventually 100%. *Agape* is that Kingdom energy that came to earth in the Person of Christ Incarnate. Such maturity begins to align our personality with that of God, Who is Spirit. God is *Agape;* He does not have *Agape.* It is His nature, His personality, His purpose. Consider John 10:30, "Father and I are one."

2. *Agape* Incarnate in us has been designed for the purpose of maturity. In Scripture the word maturity is the Greek word *telios* defined as *coming to the full purpose of its created intent.* Father's intent in the New Birth is the new creation or a human being in whom there has been a measurable transformation of the human personality. Maturity or the intended transformation consists of the supernatural re-alignment of our human DNA with that of God Who is *Agape. Agape* perfected (*telios)* in us is being conformed to the image of Jesus Christ (see Rom. 8:29).

3. The intimacy desired and offered by the Father, Son, and Holy Spirit engages the person who has been

called to make this spiritual journey (*klesia* in Greek is one who has been called out to follow Jesus). Such a person is being impelled and encouraged *to have a more direct encounter and less mediated relationship of intimacy with God as a Father.* As the result of *Agape,* God's Own energy, we are being mentored into the skill of aligning with God's eternal purpose in the earth (Greek: *boulema*). Thus, we are *inexorably* being moved toward intimacy with the Father identified as being a friend of God (see John 15:15 with James 2:23).

4. God describes Himself as One Who *hides* Himself (see Isa. 45:15). Christ's job description consists of taking us, by means of personality transformation, into the conscious presence of our Father Who is Spirit. The Kingdom offer to know God as our friend appears to be something like the Special Forces or Navy Seal program, intensely rigorous and demanding. Jesus said that unless we love Him more than our natural family and deny ourselves by taking up our cross and following Him, we are not worthy of Him (see Matt. 10:37–38). There are repeated experiences, some intended and others circumstantial, rooted in a fallen world that make us want to quit and go home. The demands and challenges of our spiritual journey present opportunities for us to become *offended.* What seems important to grasp is that the closer one gets to graduation, the more intense and multiplied these occasions to quit and go home seem

to occur. Intimacy with God, Who is in Himself a sweet society, takes on the value of the *treasure* in the field. We are encouraged to sell it all and buy the field or trade our valuable *pearl* in order to attain/obtain that one pearl or field in which the treasure resides. We cannot quit and go home (compare 2 Pet. 1:1-11 in light of this).

5. We have been born into the Kingdom or government of God and have been given the preparation and skills necessary to make this journey to fruitfulness and intimacy. The church has been called to steward us in that calling. The Kingdom is the metaphysical and meta-cognitive dimension of Father's will being accomplished in the earth. Thus, the Kingdom remains undefined, mysterious, and totally relational. Father's invitation for us to make this journey is stated in John 6:44, "No one can come to Me unless the *Father* who sent Me draws him." Consequently, the entire content of the New Covenant consists of strenuous mentoring requiring a daily cross and the effective yielding of one's personal sovereignty, which has been designed to keep His governmental Kingdom clean. "Flesh and blood *cannot* inherit the kingdom of God; nor does the perishable inherit the imperishable" (1 Cor. 15:50).

It is the insemination and cultivation of *Agape* that brings those called out to follow Jesus to maturity, allowing us to live in the conscious presence of our Father Who is Spirit.

Corruption and the Eternal Seed

Grace be with all those who love our Lord Jesus Christ with incorruptible love (Eph. 6:24).

For you have been born again not of seed which is perishable but imperishable, that is, through the living and enduring word of God (1 Pet. 1:23).

There is an important connection between the incorruptible eternal Seed and corruption through ungoverned desire. Let's look at this from the perspective of Matthew's story of the seed sower:

*³Behold, the sower went out to sow; ⁴and as he sowed, some seeds fell beside the road, and the birds came and **ate them up**. ⁵Others fell on the rocky places, where they did not have much soil; and immediately they sprang up, because they had no depth of soil. ⁶But when the sun had risen, they were scorched; and because they had no root, they **withered away**. ⁷Others fell among the thorns, and the thorns came up and **choked** them out. ⁸And others fell on the good soil and yielded a crop, some a hundredfold, some sixty, and some thirty (Matt. 13:3–8; also see Matt. 13:18-23).*

The eternal Seed comes under attack in several different ways. Instead of finding fertile soil it can be stolen and eaten by cute little birds, be scorched by the sun and withered by lack of water, or be unprotected and choked or crowded out by thorns. However, the eternal Seed "sown on the good soil, this is the man who hears the word and understands it; who indeed bears fruit and brings forth, some a hundredfold, some sixty, and some thirty" (Matt. 13:23). This is fruit in measurable degrees. But to reap fruit, we have to guard and protect the Seed.

The "weapons of our warfare are not of the flesh, but divinely powerful for the destruction of fortresses" (2 Cor. 10:4); therefore, we must examine the source of corruption. Jesus identifies the source as the father of the lie in John 8:44, "You are of your father the devil, and you want to do the desires of your father. He was a murderer from the beginning, and does not stand in the truth because there is no truth in him. Whenever he speaks a lie, he speaks from his own nature, for he is a liar and the father of lies." So the source of corruption is the false father of the lie and the cause of corruption is wanting to please or obey this false father.

In what form did the lie come to you? There are many ways we can buy the lie and expose the eternal Seed:

- Philosophical. Philosophy means love of wisdom, but the source of wisdom must be carefully determined so that we are not buying lies but Truth that leads to freedom.

- Doctrinal/religious. A commitment to false denominational distinctives can lead to buying into a lie. Protecting the Seed so that it can produce fruit means we follow Truth.
- Behavioral. Choosing to give an improper response to a presenting circumstance means we cannot properly respond to the Kingdom value system of producing fruit 30, 60, 100 fold. The Seed has no ground in which to take root so it withers away.
- Psychological. Refusal to believe as true all that passes through our mind. As we know, corruption is spontaneous. If we meet someone new and we think "this guy doesn't like me," it probably is not the truth. We must refuse to accept as valid every thought that runs through our mind.
- Systems. World systems seek to not only control us but direct our behavior. Giving into their rule and dominion is doing the will/wishes of the false father.
- False science/antagonism. Academic authority that proceeds from a false foundation or premise is buying the lie.
- Materialism. Being wrongly committed to the physical compared the metaphysical and spiritual.

Possess, Acquire and Control

There are innumerable variations of the illegal attempt to corrupt but they all boil down to *possess, acquire,* and *control.* When these three are encouraged or unbridled, the momentum and velocity of the *eros* shift (see Appendix for *Eros* Shift Diagram) significantly increases. The temptation in the wilderness (see Matt. 4:3-10) was an attempt to corrupt the Son of God in the same three ways:

Possess: *Bread*, turning the stones to bread is corrupting the supernatural for personal advantage.

Acquire: *Temple*, dancing on the temple roof is the corruption of using the supernatural to enhance my own personal reputation

Control: *World Kingdoms*, the offer of all the kingdoms of the world is a corruption of all that is political for the purpose of illegal rule and control.

Corruption begins at any elementary level by seeking to gain entrance at any portal. Most often, it comes in an unsophisticated manner. The result is the insertion of seeds of corruption that are like having a monkey on your back; they hang on even when you don't want them, damaging and injuring the vessel and distorting of the image of God. *Eros*, in a manner similar to *Agape*, becomes more effective as it matures. We can see the full maturation of corruption in John 3:19 and 20 in that we "*Agape* darkness."

Corruption, in the form of *eros* exercised as *possess, acquire,* and *control,* is energized by the 12 aspects of darkness defined by George McDonald[5] and by the satanic "Five I Will's"[6] that seek to overcome

[5] See "12 Aspects of Darkness" by George MacDonald in Appendix.

[6] "But you said in your heart, 'I will ascend to heaven; I will raise my throne above the stars of God, And I will sit on the mount

and corrupt the eternal Seed. In light of the fact that the eternal Seed is incorruptible, the attack is directed toward the vessel into which Seed has been inseminated—you and me. Temptation, then is seen as repeated attempts to corrupt the vessel, denying God the Father the glory due Him as the source of eternal good. Temptations are seasonal and repetitive. They are also sophisticated and appear deceptively benign. There is a direct connection between temptation and corruption: Temptation is a bird flying over your head; corruption is allowing it to make a nest in your hair!

The entire Epistle of Galatians and especially Chapter 5 could be interpreted in the light of Christ, the eternal Seed, Who was received by faith (see Gal. 3:3). If you depart from this Seed (see Gal. 5:3), you will be exposed to corruption in a manner with which you may not be prepared. When you are fallen from Christ, Who is the sole influence and source of incorruption, nothing, including religion, will help you. Corruption, identified in Galatians 5, distorts us:

> *19Now the deeds of the flesh are evident, which are: immorality, impurity, sensuality, 20idolatry, sorcery, enmities, strife, jealousy, outbursts of anger, disputes, dissensions, factions, 21envying, drunkenness, carousing, and things like these, of which I forewarn you, just as I have forewarned*

of assembly In the recesses of the north. 'I will ascend above the heights of the clouds; I will make myself like the Most High'" (Is. 14:13–14).

you, that those who practice such things will not inherit the kingdom of God (Gal. 5:19–21).

Unfaithfulness to Christ and His Seed distorts and perverts the Kingdom value system. *Agape compromised* allows us to see into the depth of the seven deadly sins set forth below. Timothy summarizes them as *"an unhealthy craving"* (1 Tim. 6:4-5 ESV). Note the sequence of the seven deadly sins that Dr. Meyers[7] sets out and the predicted results:

Personal worth/Value	corrupted into	PRIDE
Emulate/Mentoring	corrupted into	ENVY
Righteous Indignation	corrupted into	ANGER
Godly Desire	corrupted into	LUST
Normal Appetite	corrupted into	GLUTTONY
Gratification/Satisfaction	corrupted into	GREED
Contentment/Rest	corrupted into	SLOTH

The progression of corruption seems to go something like this:

Creation—God breathed into Adam and Eve.

First Adam—Adam and Eve disobeyed God and the world was corrupted.

Last Adam—God breathed into the incorruptible Christ.

New Creation—Christ breathed the incorruptible Seed into the disciples.

---

[7] Dr. Robin Meyers (1952). *Virtue in the Vice: Finding Seven Lively Virtues in the Seven Deadly Sins. Health Communications, Deerfield Beach, FL.*

Conflict Surrounding the Seed

Grace be with all those who love our Lord Jesus Christ with incorruptible love (Eph. 6:24).

The eternal Seed is incorruptible but *eros* makes repeated attempts to corrupt the vessel into which the eternal Seed has been breathed. Confidence, then, must be placed in the fruit of the eternal Seed, not in the vessel (see Gal. 2:20). The eternal Seed must be guarded, protected, nourished, watered, and cultivated so that Christ can be formed in us (see Gal. 4:19). In Christ we become progressively less corruptible and less temptable, not out of human effort or legalism but as the result of the *cultivation* of the eternal Seed. In this, we are approaching Paul's desire that we "love our Lord Jesus Christ with an *incorruptible love [Agape]*" (Eph. 6:24).

Corruption causes conflict around the *vessel* into which the Seed has been planted resulting in it being interrupted, arrested, suspended, or plunged into confusion and darkness. This conflict happens in several different ways:

    a. **Stolen.** Before I understood and could respond, the Seed was forgotten or ignored. The Kingdom simply failed to take root in my life.

b. Trampled. Attempting to live by the Kingdom value system results in conflicting voices, religious politics, and multiplicity of doctrines that trample all over the Seed.

c. Shallow. Insufficient depth causes the sun to dry the roots of the Seed and cause it to wither.

d. Crowded. The tyranny of the urgent causes other things to press in corrupting the Kingdom priority. This is not necessarily overt sin; good things can cause displaced affection.

In order to govern our desires, God gave us the Person of Jesus Christ Who behaved in a manner that pleased His Father. He carried the DNA of God and came to earth as the eternal, uncreated Seed and in death and resurrection He inseminated us with Himself with the intention that the Seed would find fertile soil and grow. His death, burial, and resurrection give Him the capacity to come to us in spiritual form so that we can be "rooted and grounded in love" (Eph. 3:17-18). As we embrace and cultivate the Seed, fruitfulness comes in *measurable* degrees 30%, 60%, 100%. This guarantees that our Kingdom inheritance is safe, productive, and fruitful.

The rich young ruler didn't ask Jesus how to get saved. He had kept all the commands; he wanted to know what he needed to do to be 100% fruitful. Jesus explained to him that he had to govern his love for money and material things, but he wasn't willing to do that. Ungoverned desire ruled him and Jesus exposed it in an attempt to set him free from corruption.

How the Seed is Implanted

Unlike Adam and Eve who threw us into corruption, Christ was fully governed. He was our example, and we are unable to mature without Him as our foundation. In the wilderness, Christ had three opportunities to conduct Himself in an ungoverned manner, but He didn't respond in a corrupt manner to any of the temptations. It is Christ Who enables us to be free from ungoverned desires and corruption. He imparted to us an incorruptible Seed of *Agape* that grows and matures in us, freeing us from corruption. Understanding just how this eternal Seed functions in setting us free is critical. It can be summarized with what I call the "Four C's."

Conception	Insemination of Eternal Seed	New Birth
Content	Response to Value System	New Creation
Conflict	Attempt to corrupt the vessel	New Warfare
Corruption	Inseminated Seed is Eternal and Incorruptible	New Israel

Perhaps a summary of the process will help make this clear: I was impregnated (Conception) with the content of a new value system—the Seed (Content). That content caused warfare (Conflict) in an attempt to corrupt the Seed before it came to birth (Corruption). However, the Seed is incorruptible so corruption is defeated. As an uncorrupted member of His body, I become effective in breaking the power of corruption within my personal sphere and am instrumental in setting creation free.

Because the eternal Seed is the uncreated, Incarnate Son Who came in the form of *Agape* Incarnate and became to us the mirror image of God, He is *incapable* of being corrupted. He gives Himself to us as the eternal Seed, the DNA of which is *total and complete obedience* to Father's will/wishes. Of Him Father declared that He is "well pleased" (Matt. 3:17). And, it is Christ as the eternal Seed Who "dwells in our hearts by faith" (Eph. 3:17), making us pleasing to God in the same way. He chose by death and resurrection to impart Himself to us as *pure Spirit, pure Light, and pure Agape in the form of the eternal Seed* to be received, prioritized, cultivated, and protected. This is the treasure in the field for which we sell it all and the pearl of great price for which we trade everything.

Jesus became the eternal, uncreated, and incorruptible Seed by means of His willingness to empty Himself, be faithful unto death, even death on the Cross, and be resurrected. In this Seed is perfect obedience. In this Seed is the hope for the entire universe. In this Seed is the new creation apart from which all is corrupt. In this Seed is all that could ever be needed or desired. Like the acorn and the oak tree, God's DNA provided for every contingency and possible human expectation in the eternal Seed of His Son.

The insemination of that eternal Seed into the corrupted human vessel is called the New Birth and it involves conflict. Other than Christ and Paul, Luther may have been the bravest man in church history because he stood without compromise. Had he compromised a quarter inch, the power of the monolith of the Roman Catholic Church of that day would not have been broken. The same is true in Christ and in Paul. When that is true in you and me, it breaks the power of any system. That New Birth is nothing less than a new creation. Perfect obedience, in the form of an incorruptible Seed has been placed into a corrupted/corruptible human being and perfect obedience now abides within us. Father's *Agape* now expressed as Christ's *Agape* is understood as the *transcendent* becoming *immanent* for the purpose of God's will being done on the earth as it is in heaven.

Thus, the Kingdom can be understood in three sequences:

Transcendent becoming immanent is the New Jerusalem coming down (see Rev. 3:12). The promise of the Father was that God would send His Spirit (see John 14:26), and He did this out of covenantal faithfulness.

Immanent becoming replicated as Christ is formed in *Agape* activity (see Gal. 4:19). Light as the Kingdom narrative came to us in faithfulness, exposing darkness and creating a love for Truth.

Agape replicated is the Kingdom transformation of Matthew 5:43-48 whereby we become perfect as our Father is perfect. Father's love replicated results in the promise of the Father that "all of the families of the earth shall be blessed" (Acts 3:25). All of creation is released from corruption into the freedom intended by God the Father. *Agape* as Father's DNA and glory results in a taker becoming a giver. This is the glory of God and He accomplished this mystery by means of the New Birth—placing the eternal, uncreated, and incorruptible Seed into a corruptible vessel and transforming that vessel into a replication of His Own *Agape* (see 1 John 4:8-19). We give God the glory He is due as corruptible vessels learn to love God incorruptibly!

Wrong allegiance or misplaced affection toward anyone or anything other than the sovereign God results in forms of spiritual blindness and deafness. Workouts in Father's gymnasium involve our being exercised in these same three spheres: In the Spirit by learning to walk, think, and be discerning; in light by exposing darkness and all that is self-referential; and in *Agape* by learning to be pure givers, ceasing unbridled taking.

Setting Creation Free from Corruption

> [19]*For the anxious longing of the creation waits eagerly for the revealing of the sons of God.* [20]*For the creation was subjected to futility, not willingly, but because of Him who subjected it, in hope* [21]*that the creation itself also will be set free from its slavery to corruption into the freedom of the glory of the children of God (Rom. 8:19–21).*

Note the two words *futility* and *corruption*. Who subjected the universe to vanity, futility, corruption? God did—for a purpose. We blame it on the devil, but creation was made subject to futility before the foundation of the whole creation. Satan was not the first cause; Father decided to allow creation to embrace futility and corruption. These two words had me bouncing a bit because Father did this in hope. The hope is verse 21: freedom for the children of God. His hope was that creation itself would be delivered from the bondage of corruption or decay. He is going to do that by choosing a people of His Own who love Him incorruptibly and the freedom that they enjoy is going to set the whole creation free. Christ was without sin, but He had to be tested to come to full maturity as a Man. He was tested and found sinless, consequently our help came from outside. Nothing in the earth could do this for us except God came to us as *Agape* Incarnate. But that *Agape* has to be tested in us in order to be brought to maturity. It is the testing that perfects us.

Futility is planting carrots and getting weeds. It can be as simple as intending to say the right thing to someone and ending up saying it twisted or in anger. Every one of us have felt futility because the entire creation is subjected to it. Corruption came into the world and Christ came to teach us how to love Him without corruption. When we do, we are set free and can then set the entire creation free to enjoy the freedom that we have experienced.

Corruption and incorruption have to do with being governed or ungoverned. We are to give ourselves for an incorruptible and unfading "crown of glory" (1 Pet. 5:4), not a corruptible one. The whole creation is waiting for God's people to find out how freedom actually works.

Incorruption is used in many places in Scripture. Suppose we reverse the process of corruption and actually saw incorruption sweep over our nation? Paul saw the glory of God in the face of Christ and was ready to suffer for it. He even said that whatever suffering he endured was not even to be compared with what is to be revealed. Paul understood something about freedom. God wants to reveal the fact that He subjected the whole creation to futility knowing that in Christ the whole redemptive act would emerge along with a people who would learn to obey Him. This is what Romans 8:21 is saying—the sons of God will be set free from the slavery of corruption that continually eats at them, and they in turn will set all of creation free. Creation waits to discover what we are looking at right now! We know this because Romans 8:22 says that "the whole creation groans and suffers the pains of child birth together." Creation groans, we groan, and the Holy Spirit groans. God uses all things to conform us to His image and teach us to govern our desires because there's purpose in it all—to set creation free! Don't ever think you are just going to be saved and get out of here. The freedom that you are now carrying is what sets creation free. It has to be that way because Christ bought that freedom for us. He was the freedom, and He gave that freedom to you and me. The Body of Christ has to be the freedom for the world. We are the answer—as long as we are in the world we are the light of the world (see Matt 5:14). What we are doing here is not a drill. Father's purpose is serious, and it has unfolding effects on the nations.

To function in our role of setting creation free, we must see corruption for what it is. We must define it, understand the differences between corruption and incorruption, deal with our presuppositions, and then see how it works in Scripture and in our daily lives.

It Is Finished

When Jesus had received the sour wine, He said, It is finished! And He bowed His head and gave up His spirit (John 19:30 AMP).

Therefore if any person is [ingrafted] in Christ (the Messiah) he is a new creation (a new crea-

ture altogether); the old [previous moral and spiritual condition] has passed away. Behold, the fresh and new has come! (2 Cor. 5:17 AMP).

Our love and propensity for corruption is so strong that we cannot free ourselves, and God was required to finish the task Himself. Thus, Christ's words on the Cross, *"It is finished"* takes on added weight and significance.[8] It is not about our personal salvation like we have been taught; it refers to a new King being established. The old governmental system is brought down, and a new Kingdom centered on His Kingship is established. This new government includes our salvation but is not centered on it.

Paul said that freedom of creation is the incorruptibility that is ours when corruption has been exposed and conquered (see Rom. 8:21). Because the seed we receive is incorruptible, as we love (*Agape*) the Lord Jesus in an incorruptible manner; the battle over corruption is won. The warfare surrounds the eternal Seed itself in the vessel in which it has been inseminated, and we can lose a battle without losing the war. The new creation of the Kingdom is totally and completely established on the *incorruptibility* of the eternal Seed. "It is finished" means that what God has done cannot be undone or modified by corruption. *Agape* is God's final triumph because God is *Agape*. He

---

[8]For further insight and application, I recommend *Christians and the New Creation* by Paul S. Minear, published by Westminster, John Knox Press.

doesn't have *Agape*; He IS *Agape*. If God subjected the world to futility, He knows the beginning from the end, and the end is guaranteed.

In preparation for God shaking all that can be shaken, including things on earth and in the heavenlies (see Heb. 12:26), we are in urgent need of building our life and future on the *nature of God—the DNA of His very Person.* That Person was revealed in Fathers' self-revelation at the Incarnation as Jesus stated: "If you have seen Me, you have seen the Father!" (John 14:9).

- God is Spirit: Pure Spirit, metaphysical, His presence is like the wind

- God is Light: Pure Light, essence of creation; in Him there is no darkness at all

- God is *Agape*: Pure   *Agape*,   pure   giver, incorruptible

This transcendent God (I AM) chose to become immanent, clothing Himself with human flesh. Scripture says simply that "*God* was in Christ, reconciling the world to Himself" (2 Cor. 5:19).

- Pure Spirit assumes human clothing and we beheld His glory

- Pure Light waits to be seen and embraced; waits for reception

- Pure *Agape* offers Himself as incorruptible Seed; Light and Life

The *corruption* precipitated by the following seven spheres, comes into view when we examine the concept of God's glory. When seen as temptation, appeals designed to corrupt, compromise one's affection, or cause one to be unfaithful to our Bridegroom take on a different light. What impresses me is that nothing on this list takes on the stigma associated with debauchery and prolificacy that is generally associated with corruption. Why do you call Me "Lord" if all these other things determine your behavior? We are attempting to discern the first causes:

a. Philosophical

b. Doctrinal/religious

c. Behavioral/self-will

d. Psychological

e. System; control and influence

f. False Science/antagonism

g. Materialism

All seven of these should be evaluated as the fruit of a ruling system; the strength, effort, and determination exerted toward their goal to possess, acquire, and control is underestimated. Their source of corruption is designed to contaminate and then damage the vessel in which the glory of God has been inseminated. That glory is the eternal Seed—*Agape* Incarnate replicated and displayed to the hurting world through the agency of corrupted men and women who, in the *reception* of the eternal Seed, have been transformed. This transformation occurs by our identifying and defeating the sources of corruption and personally embracing the *eros/Agape* conversion so that we can love incorruptibly. *Agape* exposes corruption, it reveals illegal and compulsive *eros* motivations and allegiances that are not Kingdom centered.

We are restating the redemptive act focusing on the eternal Seed rather than the vessel. Both are necessary, but it is the eternal Seed in which we must place our confidence and hope. The vessel suffering compromise is the theme of the Song of Solomon. Our affections can be turned in upon ourselves, used against the Bridegroom, and amazingly enough, against the Creator Himself. What the Kingdom depends upon is the uncreated, eternal, and unshakable Seed that has been inseminated into our deepest person. It, in itself, is Spirit, Light, and *Agape*.

Each season of growth and progress is exposed to new forms of temptation and renewed appeals to all that is self-referential. These strenuous, laborious, exhausting appeals to possess, acquire, and control repetitiously present themselves for us to compromise and corrupt the vessel and detract from the glory of God (see 1 Cor. 3:16-17). Incorruptibility is then dependent upon our understanding and abiding in the Person of Christ rather than in ourselves. Loss of the Seed as compared to 30% or 60% fruitfulness is a commentary on the success of the corruption or incorruption of the Seed. Bearing 100% fruit means *Agape* has been brought to full maturity and Christ is fully formed in the believer.

To set our goal to love God in a manner that is incorruptible takes on significance that is highly motivating. It involves vocational suffering; repeated repentance and adjustments, often at great cost; and the conscious choice to become a Father-pleaser.

The New Birth in Kingdom perspective suggests that Father intends to exercise His governmental influence on the earth as it is in heaven by the calling and transformation of those who have been deeply corrupted by the world system. This is why publicans and harlots will enter the Kingdom before those who are religious. In the Old Testament type, He took them out of Egypt and across Jordan, which is representative of water baptism and entry into the Promised Land. He speaks in the prophetic perfect that we are *complete* in Christ, meaning the Seed is incorruptible, and we are the winner. He centers the corrupted vessel, in whom is the eternal Seed, upon the Cross of Jesus Christ, knowing that this Cross will expose and defeat the seven sources of corruption, releasing us from being consummate, self-referential takers. He delivers us from the corruption of possess, acquire, and control and produces in us, incrementally and progressively, the Kingdom value system of *Agape*, which is untemptable, incorruptible, and unshakable.

We who have come to believe on the Person of Christ experience the transformation and spiritual dimension of the New Birth, emerge from the waters of baptism as a new creation, and are constantly and repeatedly being exposed to the attempts of darkness to compromise the vessel in which the eternal Seed has been inseminated. The appeal, as revealed in the three temptations of Christ—bread, temple, and world kingdoms—places this attempt at compromise in the sphere of that which is *seen,* meaning all that has the ability to capture the senses. Eve saw that it was "good for food; delight to the eyes; desirable to make one wise" (Gen. 3:6). When influenced by all that is satanic and demonic, *eros* is mature and skilled at things that appeal to the eye-gate.

Because *Agape* is Father's nature, it is inclined toward that which is hidden (not ostentatious) and unseen. Think of Jesus' instructions for the disciples to "tell no man" (Matt. 16:19). That which is seen is temporal; that which is unseen is eternal. How consistent this is with faith being the "assurance of *things* hoped for, the conviction of things not seen" (Heb. 11:1). Maturity expects that we, in whom the eternal Seed resides, come to fruitfulness so that we can follow Jesus and obey Him in an incorruptible manner.

John 3:16 shows us that God loved the whole world cosmos and all the people trapped in the world system. He loved it so much that He gave His Son to redeem it. Following His baptism, Jesus acknowledged being in conflict with all the ruling systems: His natural family, culture and tradition, economic entities, political entities, and the ruling powers of religion. Religion in one form or another rules the world. Jesus would not allow any aspect of the world system, including His Own mother (see Mark 3:32-33) to govern Him. To paraphrase Luke 6:46, He said, "Why do you call Me 'Lord' when all the systems govern you?"

Corruption and Our Inheritance

By having the eyes of your heart flooded with light, so that you can know and understand the hope to which He has called you, and how rich is His glorious inheritance in the saints (His set-apart ones) (Eph. 1:18 AMP).

Cultivation of the *incorruptible* Seed preserves and protects, motivates, and cleanses. The Church is teaching about getting our inheritance, but what God is asking for is His inheritance. Our job description is to give Father His inheritance. That changes everything. The moment we start thinking that our job description is to give Father His inheritance, we are on our way out of the *eros* phenomenon. We can stop thinking about heaven and hell so much because that isn't the issue. If you are a believer and you die, you have to go to heaven—there is no place else to go. Heaven is a destiny not a goal. The real issue is whether or not we are governed, have learned to be a Father-pleaser, and are able to give God His inheritance. Departure from the effects and fruit of the Seed will cause you to lose your inheritance similar to Israel losing theirs (see Matt. 21:43). They *corrupted* themselves at great expense to themselves and God's purpose (see Ezk. 16:47). The incorruptible Seed is the hope of the future—"Christ (incorruptible Seed) in you (plural), the hope of glory" (Col. 1:27).

Decisions are the critical issue. It comes down to making a choice to go to the exercise class when everything in us rebels and does not want to do it. In one parable Jesus tells of one son who says, "I will go" and does not; the other says "I will not go" and then does. Proper response is much more than verbal; it is the joy of *pleasing* the Father. Making the hard decision is the fruit of *Agape* known as *self-control* (see Gal. 5:23). Decisions or proper responses are what facilitates our movement toward *freedom* and usefulness in Father's governmental realm. All Kingdom decisions should be defined as the proper response to Father's expectation. Father will forgive us 7 times 70, but He will *not* and *cannot* cease to move us toward the freedom that is ours by right of our Kingdom inheritance. It is a shock for believers to discover that repeated forgiveness is not the primary issue in a Kingdom lifestyle; it is giving God His inheritance. The consequences of refusal or failure to give Father a proper response is loss of one's Kingdom *inheritance.* We are not loved less, but we are *used* less; leading to our having become essentially useless to the Kingdom purpose. This can be seen most clearly in Matthew 21:43, "Therefore I say to you, the kingdom of God will be taken away from you and given to a people...." We are refused the privilege to participate in that which Father is doing in the earth.

Nothing brings Father more joy than to see His Own kids embracing and living by *Agape.* Proper response is what leads us to discover, like the treasure in the field, that we are becoming Father's *inheritance* (see Eph. 1:18).

It is fully possible that the present working of the Holy Spirit is for the preparation of the divine seed bed. The delivery system of the Kingdom is more like a bumble bee depositing pollen than an aluminum salesman hocking his wares. After all, we asked for an oak tree, and He gave us an acorn.

Lying Against the Truth

But if you have bitter jealousy and selfish ambition in your heart, do not be arrogant and so lie against the truth (Jam. 3:14).

You and I are fully capable of lying against the truth. The motive for such action is *vanity* and *corruption* emerging from the darkness of the *eros* prison. When I suspect that the truth of the Kingdom may *disrupt* my foundation, the *cost* of that disruption begins to magnify in my mind and emotion. To *lie against the truth is* to cease to follow Him in order to preserve our present foundation. The consequence is clear: my light begins turning to darkness and in Matthew 6:23 Jesus said, "How great is that darkness." This could signify a strengthening of the walls of the *eros* prison.

It is perfectly possible, maybe even probable, that the Lord would set in motion certain events for the purpose of disrupting the foundational systems that He sees as illegally ruling us...*the same foundations that we are determined to defend and protect against the God of the universe.* This shows us how *vanity/corruption* moves into the Church and religious world by means of selfish ambition or vain conceit and does so with rapidity and force. This principle works in the secular world of the philosopher, the scientist, the medical field, the author, or anyone who was trying to create or preserve an image. When we are about to be embarrassed or *not look good*, it is almost a given that we could or would *lie against the Truth*. Once we understand the trap and can see the exit and freedom[9] we become willing to embrace the principles of that government to which we have committed at great personal expense.

I am totally convinced philosophically that there is no exit from the *eros* phenomenon without the New Birth. I know people come to the New Birth many ways, but once *Agape* awakens in me it is that value

---

[9]For more information on the topic of the trap and exit, read the Plumbline *The Trap, Exit, and Reward* available at Lifechangers or on Amazon or Barnes and Noble.

system that Father is interested in, not church. Lying against the truth is departure from the Kingdom value system.

In this light, to *deny* Him (see Matt. 10:33) does not affect our salvation nor His love for us but it is a *governmental* type of treason. For example, Peter's denial of Christ was a major failure and needed Jesus' direct intervention to clean up the issue. Peter helps us see *denial* as governmental failure. Just think about how many times deny/denial is used in the four gospels and the rest of the New Testament. Once we can identify the crucial enemy and principal issue, we can defeat the all-powerful self-deception and find the exit out into the freedom to which the Kingdom calls us. In order to know freedom, we must *first* acknowledge that we are in a prison. Kingdom repentance then becomes governmental and not redemptive.

The freedom promised us is truth that sets us free. This *governmental* freedom is a central issue of the New Testament and reveals Father reaching for a people of His Own. To love God and receive the Truth brought to us in Jesus defines the exit and provides that "escape [by flight] from the moral decay (rottenness and corruption) that is in the world because of covetousness (lust and greed)" (2 Pet. 1:4 AMP). From this insight into the Kingdom there are several implications that should be noted:

- Freedom does not come from either the right or the left. Freedom comes from the third choice; remaining on the *Agape* road whatever that may cost or imply. This includes church/secular issues as well as capitalism/communism/socialism issues.

- Kingdom, when seen governmentally, results in becoming a Father-Pleaser. It has been my experience that in the religious world our tendency is seek to please others. This is not freedom and once we see the prison and find the exit, we can emerge into the governmental freedom Father intended—the desire and ability to *walk with a clean conscience.* It is not for any one person or group; it is vertical and expresses our desire to please Father and honor the manner in which His government functions. This seems to be David's heart in Psalm 51:8, "Make me to hear joy and gladness *and* be satisfied; let the bones which You have broken rejoice."

- The necessity for us to develop and present *filial morality* becomes an absolute. There is no Temple in the New Jerusalem because Christ is the Light of all nations. Father is All in All; therefore, in some manner yet undiscovered, there must emerge some form of governmental clarity that is practical and workable for all peoples of all nations in all circumstances.

- "Follow Me" is the pattern for all Kings and Priests for that is the Father's established pattern. When we are aware of His eternal purposes, we are motivated to walk clean in that governmental sense, knowing that failure or refusal to do so will eventually lead to the loss of our governmental inheritance.

- It is not possible to walk clean apart from the Kingdom motive, which is centered in breaking *eros* and cleansing the ambition and manipulation that pervades all of its activity.

- The loss of one's Kingdom commission as lost inheritance may not necessarily cause the loss of one's spiritual insight and anointing because the gifts and calling of God are irrevocable and are not dependent on repentance. However, the relational intimacy of being a Father-Pleaser and walking clean in a governmental sense has been lost or abandoned. "But I have this [one charge to make] against you: that you have left (abandoned) the love that you had at first [you have deserted Me, your first love]" (Rev. 2:4).

Incorruptibility is *Agape* Reformation

If it were not so, I would have told you (Jn. 14:2).

Grace be with all those who love our Lord Jesus Christ with incorruptible love (Eph. 6:24).

The restoration of *Agape* is essential to reformation. *Agape* alone can become the rallying cry to release the impetus that the living God alone controls: "For to everyone who has, more shall be given, and he will have an abundance" (Matt. 25:29). The eternal Seed implanted in each of us carries the intent that *Agape* be brought to maturity. This suggests that the

Kingdom equation, which includes incorruptibility, can be stated in this progression:

- *Agape* Seed restores the image of the Father to creation, allowing us to mature and enjoy the freedom Father intended, and produces Kingdom fruit.
- Kingdom fruit is incorruptibility and *arrival of the New Jerusalem.*
- The New Jerusalem is the government of the Kingdom from above that is "not of this world" (Jn. 18:36).
- Kingdom government allows incorruptible *Agape* to mature in us so that the will of God is done on the earth as it is in Heaven. *Agape* is Christ's hidden source of life and strength that is available to us.

Jesus' statement, *"If this were not so, I would have told you"* (Jn. 14:2) could be identified as *incorruptible speech* because it was totally absent of *eros*. My sense is that those who are immature, with the eternal Seed uncultivated, are incapable of incorruptible speech and behavior. Thus, the Kingdom is purely supernatural. We are simply unable to mature (Greek *telios*) in *Agape* until we can give an *incorruptible* response to circumstances of injustice and inequality that Father allows in our sphere. This is another way of restating the principle that "all things work together for good to those who love God" (Rom. 8:28).

Cyclical and unending repetition of a present

circumstance, like Israel's 40-year journey around the same mountain in the wilderness (or what I call another lap around the mountain), is due to our ignorance or failure/refusal to give a mature, *incorruptible Agape response* to an event or set of circumstances. Surrendering to that which is not to our liking causes diminishment and eventually death to corruption. *Agape* takes us out of *prolonged infancy* (Greek *napioi,* Heb. 5:13) and behaviors such as vain or empty glory, provoking one another, and envy.

When the entire Body of Christ remains in infancy, the *eros* shift increases (see *Eros* Shift Diagram in Appendix), due to the fact that the Body of Christ is designed to be the guidance system like the sun, moon, and stars for this present generation.

These principles of incorruptible *Agape* reveal *eros* as the source of our behaving in a corrupted manner. Incorruptible *Agape* compels us to speak, think, and act in truth. Truth-ing one another in *Agape* is the eternal Seed producing its Kingdom fruit as illustrated in 2 Cor. 4:1-2, "We have renounced the things hidden because of shame…not walking in craftiness…but by the manifestation of truth." The guiding principle is Christ's words, "If it were not true…I would have told you…."

This puts us on a course correction that leads to the *Agape culture* being restored to a hurting world. My word or a hand-shake would again become something that would more closely resemble the early Christian influence our culture and schools once had. The ruling systems are then being corrected and instructed in the principles of that Kingdom in accordance with Ephesians 3:10, "so that the manifold wisdom of God might now be made known through the church to the rulers and the authorities in the heavenly places." *Eros* and corruption would be *displaced* by *Agape* being brought to maturity as the incorruptible Christ is formed within each of us. This becomes the single hope of the world: "Christ in you [plural], the hope of glory" (Col. 1:27) and out of this comes the existential reality and fulfillment of the promise given to Abraham that "in you shall all the families of the earth be blessed" (Gen. 28:14).

Desires of Your Heart

Delight yourself also in the Lord, and He will give you the desires and secret petitions of your heart (Psalm 37:4 AMP).

We sometimes interpret this verse that if we want a Mercedes, He will give us one. What this really means is that if we learn to please Him, He will change what we desire. The transformation of our desires is what leads us to freedom. In the realm of alcoholism, we know that we cannot set anyone free from that which they still love. When our desires change, our freedom follows. If the Son sets you free, you are free indeed—the deed is behavior!

When governed, our desires are born out of our relationship with the Father, and we can recognize an illegal desire. There is a difference.

If our desire is to be a millionaire and that desire possesses us, we can become very demanding in attaining that goal. When our desires are modified, a million dollars has relative value to us because we look at things differently. Would I like to have a million dollars? Yes. Am I obsessive about it? No. That is freedom. Pleasing the Father is determined not by will power but by the actual transformation of our desires. Being set free requires our desires to be changed. Corruption in advertising creates an unsatisfied desire to have the Mercedes. When I get free from that desire, we are free to own one because it doesn't own us. We are free.

Understanding that our governed desires are from Father can turn our prayer life into a life of prayer. Father's desire in us awakens us in the middle of the night to intercede for a few moments. You'll know whether your prayer life has life in it. As long as it does, keep doing it. If you come to a period when it changes, be brave and make the transition. We become continually at His service and open to whatever He wants. At unusual times He might prompt you to give someone $20. When our desires are governed, His prompts are a natural two-way conversation. Like a horse that is neck reigned, as soon as the leather touches our neck we know what to do. There is no bit in our mouth that pulls and causes bleeding before we get it, a simple touch is enough.

The Lord wants to use our governed desires and

give us opportunities to set creation free. I think some of the religious stuff we do is like playing in kindergarten, and we just continue doing it our entire life. Kindergarten is designed to move us from the elementary to a deeper degree of maturity.

One of my friends was really into Christian music. One day he got in the car to make a 3.5 hour road trip and the Lord said, "Leave the music off." By the time he arrived, the presence of God was so strong in the car he could hardly stand it. He realized that the music was a crutch because he couldn't stand the quiet. When we live out of routine rather than open-hearted response, we're often afraid that we'll miss or fail to do something. Growing up is not mystical, it is quite practical.

When a couple is first married they say to their spouse, "I love you, and I will never leave you." Their spouse responds, "I will never leave you, either!" Fifty years later you don't have to keep saying that because both know that neither of them are going anywhere. The comfort level has increased. Like a couple who has been together a long time, you and God can almost finish each other's sentences. When our desires are governed, we are free to be who God intended when He created us. If we're not doing something right, He'll let us know, but we certainly don't need to fear omitting things. It really is His responsibility to let us know.

When Judith and I were living in Ft. Lauderdale, I was out of town visiting with some friends one time and planning to leave the following Friday. I woke up one morning and the Lord said quietly, "Change your ticket to Wednesday." I wondered why, but I got on the phone and changed the ticket strictly out of obedience. I travelled home with no problem and the following morning learned that a hurricane was headed straight for Ft. Lauderdale. All flights would have been cancelled on Friday, and Judith would have faced the hurricane by herself.

All I'm trying to say is let's enjoy the journey. Let's don't work at it or climb our way up. We don't do that in our marriage, why do it with the Lord? When our desires are governed, we can say, "It's been a good day. I've enjoyed You, Lord, and enjoyed life." It is a love affair, and the Lord will prompt us if we answer our wife or friends in an un-truthing manner. That kind of prompting is how we learn to govern our desires.

Breaking the Power of Corruption

By means of these He has bestowed on us His precious and exceedingly great promises, so that through them you may escape [by flight] from the moral decay (rottenness and corruption) that is in the world because of covetousness (lust and greed), and become sharers (partakers) of the divine nature (2 Pet. 1:4 AMP).

In my own journey corruption seemed like such an unavoidable companion that it was shocking to me to hear Peter say we could be free from the corruption that is in the world. It doesn't matter whether I drive a Ford or a Mercedes. I would prefer a Mercedes, but it really isn't an issue when the power of corruption is broken. I noticed that a friend of mine was always dressed to the nines in clothes with name brand symbols on them. When I asked him about it, he said that he didn't have enough self-worth to not have a shirt with a name brand symbol on it. His identity depended on it. Think of all the Michael Kors purses out there. Desire is dictating our behavior. It doesn't matter if we buy the purse or not, the question is do we have to have that purse or name brand label to feel whole?

My son-in-law was riding a BMW motorcycle wearing a pair of Harley motorcycle boots when someone pulled up beside him and mocked him about what he was riding. That is corruption, and it is dictating human behavior with torment. Once we know that we are free from it, we do not have go down under the guilt, pain, or pressure of corruption.

In the wilderness, Jesus encountered corruption when He was tempted to bow to the kingdoms of the world. He broke the power of the world systems with a spoken word in order to set us free. Conquering corruption through self-will means we have successfully made it to the top of the pile, but we are still not free. We're probably closer to being a religious Pharisee with the corruption tightly stuffed inside. Systems are first dealt with internally then externally. He doesn't destroy them so that we'll be free; He first sets us free internally, then He annuls the systems. Our own freedom is a prerequisite to systems of corruption being broken. Once we understand that, we're on our way to freedom! If we want to be a Kingdom citizen and a free person, we have to learn how to dismiss corruption before it even starts. Romans states:

> *[1] Therefore, [there is] now no condemnation (no adjudging guilty of wrong) for those who are in Christ Jesus, who live [and] walk not after the dictates of the flesh, but after the dictates of the Spirit. [2] For the law of the Spirit of life [which is] in Christ Jesus [the law of our new being] has freed me from the law of sin and of death (Rom. 8:1-2).*

We know this because Scripture speaks of a future when the whole world will be delivered from corruption. We are delivered through our New Birth, a governmental decree on the basis of what God gave us in Christ that allows us to dismiss acting corruptly. We no longer entertain the corruption that leads to temptation. This was illustrated when Jesus spent 40 days and 40 nights in the wilderness where He encountered the corruption in the world. Jesus never broke the power of corruption. Instead, He broke the *power of the system of corruption* as illustrated in Colossians 2:15, "[God] disarmed the principalities and powers that were ranged against us and made a bold display and public example of them, in triumphing over them in Him and in it [the cross]." Over the Cross were written the words "Jesus of Nazareth, King of the Jews" in Hebrew, Latin, and Greek. Hebrew represents religion, Latin represents business, and Greek represents philosophy. Jesus brought truth to every aspect of human society, and He counters the corruption in all three areas.

Jesus uses corruption to bring us to Himself. If we did not have corruption, we would not need Him. The fact that ugly stuff emerges from us without our knowledge or permission causes us to turn to Him and His governmental rule. If a corrupt thought suddenly appears that is against everything we know, we are being faced with temptation in order to be set free. We can press into Christ and say, "Jesus I need you." When He says that He "uses all things" for our good, corruption is one of them. We have a sovereign God who uses everything and anything to bring us to freedom. Once we are free, we can begin to set creation free.

There is an irremediable mortal wound in human nature that allows corruption access. Jesus did not deal with the corruption; He dealt with you and me. He buried us in the waters of Noah and brought us up in resurrection so that we could walk out of corruption with Him and His family.

The implications of the New Birth is freedom from corruption not the absence of it. Corruption is ubiquitous, ever-present, pervasive, unexpected, and uncontrolled. So our freedom is a personal issue not a cultural one. Christ was baptized in order to actively identify with the human condition of corruption. In Himself He was sinless, yet He was made to be sin in order to absorb and embrace human corruption so that we could be free. *What man could not do, God did! The jail cell is open ... walk out!*

We cannot pretend we are not subject to the appearance and influence of corruption, but we don't have to focus on it. If we are driving down the highway and think of driving our car head on into oncoming traffic so that all our problems would be gone, that is suicidal corruption. It happens more than anyone knows. When lustful thoughts flash in front of us, consider it an early warning system. Ignore the sudden unexpected appearances of corruption, don't pursue them. We can't pretend that we are immune to the appearance of corruption. If we say we believe the Bible so we can't be corrupted, there is a false sense of security. Freedom from corruption means ignoring temptation's sudden, unexpected appearances that are designed to take our freedom and leave us in captivity. It means governing our desires. The simple awareness of corruption is a defense mechanism allowing us to get free.

The following questions are not intended to expose anyone, just to get us thinking about our freedom or lack thereof:

- As a child or adult have I ever been corrupted? If so, you may be open to all kinds of darkness.
- Am I being mentored into a corrupt manner

of behaving? Am I learning how to cheat on my taxes and falsely represent myself?

- Do I or have I corrupted others? This may require some personal repentance and change of behavior. If some specific event comes to mind, admit to it, and get clean of it. This includes sexual issues, but involves way more than that.
- Is my church corrupt?
- Is my business corrupt or does it follow an *Agape* value system?
- Am I presently being corrupted by one or some combination of the world systems?
- Is my doctrinal emphasis corrupt?
- Do I secretly respond to corrupt images and themes? Can I recognize them?
- If I was not afraid of people, of God, of Hell, would I serve God freely?
- Have I been corrupted to the point that I feel it is vain to serve God?
- In what ways am I being mentored into Kingdom life and understanding of the power of corruption?
- Am I dealing with passive corruption? Am I the same person in my private life that I am in public? Does what I do and how I act align with the Kingdom value system of *Agape*?

Appendix

Corruption Scriptures

<u>Corruption is used 42 times in New American Standard Version</u>

Gen 6:11	Now the earth was	corrupt	in the sight of God, and the earth
Gen 6:12	on the earth, and behold, it was	corrupt	for all flesh had corrupted
Gen 6:12	it was corrupt; for all flesh had	corrupted	their way upon the earth.
Exod 32:7	up from the land of Egypt, have	corrupted	themselves.
Lev 22:25	the food of your God; for their	corruption	is in them, they have a defect,
Deut 4:16	so that you do not act	corruptly	and make a graven image for
Deut 4:25	long in the land, and act	corruptly	and make an idol in the form of
Deut 9:12	brought out of Egypt have acted	corruptly	They have quickly turned aside
Deut 31:29	that after my death you will act	corruptly	and turn from the way which I have
Deut 32:5	They have acted	corruptly	toward Him, They are not His
Judg 2:19	they would turn back and act more	corruptly	than their fathers, in following

2 Chron 26:16	heart was so proud that he acted	corruptly	and he was unfaithful to the
2 Chron 27:2	But the people continued acting	corruptly	
Neh 1:7	"We have acted very	corruptly	against You and have not kept the
Job 15:16	less one who is detestable and	corrupt	Man, who drinks iniquity like
Job 15:34	fire consumes the tents of the	corrupt	
Ps 14:1	"There is no God." They are	corrupt	they have committed abominable
Ps 14:3	aside, together they have become	corrupt	There is no one who does good,
Ps 53:1	"There is no God," They are	corrupt	and have committed abominable
Ps 53:3	together they have become	corrupt	There is no one who does good,
Eccles 7:7	makes a wise man mad, And a bribe	corrupts	the heart.
Isa 1:4	of evildoers, Sons who act	corruptly	They have abandoned the Lord,
Jer 6:28	They, all of them, are	corrupt	
Ezek 16:47	were too little, you acted more	corruptly	in all your conduct than they.

Ezek 20:44	evil ways or according to your	corrupt	deeds, O house of Israel,"
Ezek 23:11	saw this, yet she was more	corrupt	in her lust than she, and her
Ezek 28:17	up because of your beauty; You	corrupted	your wisdom by reason of your
Dan 2:9	together to speak lying and	corrupt	words before me until the
Dan 6:4	of accusation or evidence of	corruption	inasmuch as he was faithful, and
Dan 6:4	faithful, and no negligence or	corruption	was to be found in him.
Zeph 3:7	But they were eager to	corrupt	all their deeds.
Mal 2:8	by the instruction; you have	corrupted	the covenant of Levi," says the
Rom 1:23	God for an image in the form of	corruptible	man and of birds and four-footed
Rom 8:21	be set free from its slavery to	corruption	into the freedom of the glory of
1 Cor 15:33	Do not be deceived: "Bad company	corrupts	good morals."
2 Cor 7:2	we wronged no one, we	corrupted	no one, we took advantage of no
Gal 6:8	flesh will from the flesh reap	corruption	but the one who sows to the

Eph 4:22	the old self, which is being	corrupted	in accordance with the lusts of
2 Pet 1:4	divine nature, having escaped the	corruption	that is in the world by lust.
2 Pet 2:10	who indulge the flesh in its	corrupt	desires and despise authority.
2 Pet 2:19	they themselves are slaves of	corruption	for by what a man is overcome,
Rev 19:2	judged the great harlot who was	corrupting	the earth with her immorality, and

12 Aspects of Darkness

These points are from George McDonald

a. I am my own. I am my own king and my own subject.

b. I am the center from which go out my thoughts.

c. I am the object and the end of my thoughts; back upon *me* as the alpha and omega of life, my thoughts return.

d. My own glory is, and ought to be, my chief care.

e. My ambition, to gather the regards of men to the one center.

f. My pleasure is my pleasure.

g. My kingdom is as many as I can bring to acknowledge my greatness over them.

h. My judgment is the faultless rule of things.

i. My rights are what I desire.

j. The more I am all in all to myself, the greater I am.

k. The less I acknowledge debt or obligation to another; the more I close my eyes to the fact that I did not make myself; the more self-sufficing I feel or *imagine* myself the greater I am.

l. I will be free with the freedom that consists in doing whatever I am inclined to do, from what ever quarter may come the inclination. To do my own will so long as I feel anything to be my will, is to be free, to live." [10]

---

[10] George MacDonald (2004). *Creation in Christ: Unspoken Sermons*, Kingship, pg. 140.

Eros Shift Chart
Galatians 1:4

An *agape*-motivated culture

Governed Desires
Human desires under the influence of Judeo-Christian tradition or Christian culture rooted in *agape*.

Reformation in Reverse—Once society is out of control, broken loose, unstrained or unbridled, consequences are inevitable.

An *eros*-motivated culture

Ungoverned Desires
Human desires under the influence of a culture driven by *eros*.

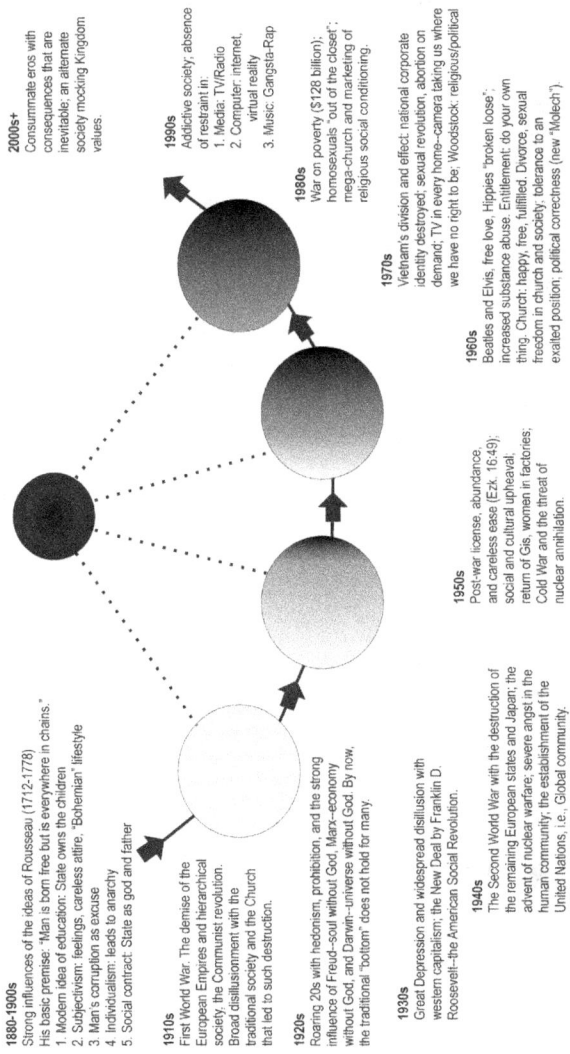

1880-1900s
Strong influences of the ideas of Rousseau (1712-1778)
His basic premise: "Man is born free but is everywhere in chains."
1. Modern idea of education: State owns the children
2. Subjectivism: feelings, careless attire, "Bohemian" lifestyle
3. Man's corruption as excuse
4. Individualism: leads to anarchy
5. Social contract: State as god and father

1910s
First World War. The demise of the European Empires and hierarchical society, the Communist revolution. Broad disillusionment with the traditional society and the Church that led to such destruction.

1920s
Roaring 20s with hedonism, prohibition, and the strong influence of Freud—soul without God, Marx-economy without God, and Darwin—universe without God. By now, the traditional "bottom" does not hold for many.

1930s
Great Depression and widespread disillusion with western capitalism; the New Deal by Franklin D. Roosevelt—the American Social Revolution.

1940s
The Second World War with the destruction of the remaining European states and Japan; the advent of nuclear warfare; severe angst in the human community, the establishment of the United Nations, i.e. Global community.

1950s
Post-war license, abundance, and careless ease (Ezk. 16:49); social and cultural upheaval: return of GIs, women in factories; Cold War and the threat of nuclear annihilation.

1960s
Beatles and Elvis, free love, Hippies "broken loose"; increased substance abuse. Entitlement: do your own thing. Church: happy, free, fulfilled. Divorce, sexual freedom in church and society, tolerance to an exalted position: political correctness (new "Molech").

1970s
Vietnam's division and effect; national corporate identity destroyed; sexual revolution, abortion on demand; TV in every home–camera taking us where we have no right to be: Woodstock: religious/political

1980s
War on poverty ($128 billion); homosexuals "out of the closet"; mega-church and marketing of religious social conditioning.

1990s
Addictive society; absence of restraint in:
1. Media: TV/Radio
2. Computer: internet, virtual reality
3. Music: Gangsta-Rap

2000s+
Consummate *eros* with consequences that are inevitable; an alternate society mocking Kingdom values.

Other *Plumblines* by Bob Mumford
Available through Lifechangers, Amazon or Barnes & Noble

Acting Against Myself

Acting against myself (AAM is the proper way to live our Christian life. It has to do with distinguishing between light and dark, Agape and Eros, so that we can leave the old way of life and live differently. Agape is behavioral. It isn't legal or methodical; it needs to be brought out of the court room into the family room. An Agape reformation begins by learning to act against ourselves. Agape alone expects and requires us to mature to the point of being able to give ourselves away. In Matthew 16:24-25, Jesus states this as "forgetting himself and his own interests." Christ discipled the twelve, incrementally teaching them what it meant to act against themselves. He taught them and us both by example and by biblical precept. ISBN 1-884004-94-6

It Came to Pass

Change is inevitable. In this Plumbline, Bob explains how the whole world has been plunged into rapid and intense change since the 1960s. Making course corrections can be compared to sailing; we must "tack" into change little bits at a time, often seeming to be off course even though we are heading in the right direction. A look back at the Body of Christ and historical events over the last few decades will illustrate this "tacking" process more clearly. ISBN 1-884004-95-4

Journey to the Father on the Agape Road

This Plumbline is an agridged version of the book The Agape Road and contains the essential principles of the book. From deep and agonizing personal experience, Bob shares his victory of three life-crippling hindrances: anger, a critical mouth, and free-floating anxiety. The principles that worked for him will work for you, too—no matter what private issues you may be struggling with. After years of pastoring, preaching, counseling, and writing, Bob shares how you can fulfill your destiny by escaping the seven giants of failure, learning how to rest on the Agape Road, experiencing the healing power of Agape, and discovering the joy of being a Father-pleaser. Reading Journey to the Father is like sitting at the feet of the Master, feeling His words deep in your heart, and sensing His healing power in the broken places of your life. ISBN 1-884004-98-9.

The Trap, Exit and Reward

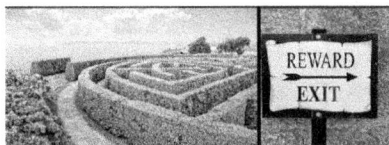

Using two stories about the trap, Bob identifies what keeps us trapped and how to get out. While we are in the trap we continually surrender our freedom for our feelings. The entire creation waits to be set free from its slavery to corruption into freedom (see Rom. 8:19-21). From 2 Peter 1, Bob shows us six steps to finding the exit and the reward: a rich and abundant welcome into the eternal kingdom of our Lord (2 Pet. 1:11) so that we can participate in setting creation free.
ISBN 978-1-940054-01-8

Feed My Sheep: 60 Years in Ministry

1954 to 2014 marks 60 years in active ministry for Bob Mumford. His story began in the Navy in a little four-bed sick bay on the USS Aludra when he began to embrace the call to teach. Feeding God's people in every nation has been his life-long commission. This story chronicles Bob's journey from meeting Christ through his Navy experience, Bible College, Charismatic Renewal, and the Covenant Movement. He shares what he has learned in following Jesus all these years. ISBN 978-1-940054-05-6

Circle of Friendship

Within the Trinity of the Father, Son, and Holy Spirit there is a circle of friendship, and we are being invited into it. When Jesus started His journey with the disciples, one of His goals was friendship—He wanted to reveal Father's secrets to them. Real friendship involves trust and intimacy, not over-familiarity. In this Plumbline, Bob gives us four ingredients common to friendship and shows us the importance of relationships being reciprocal. God is calling us into a true friendship with Himself and with others. We must accept each other just like we are and choose to surrender self-protection and control. When we center our whole being on pleasing the Father, it radically affects our ethical and moral behavior. A vital aspect of our circle of friendship with God is waiting on Him; by it we exchange our weakness for His strength. After a while, we come to a place where the poise of our soul is toward the Lord, and we can enjoy Father's presence.

Abba Father: Journey into Father's Heart

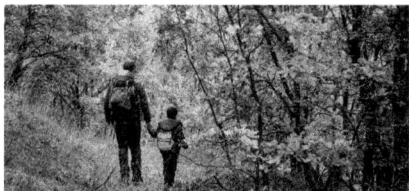

"Abba Father" is a statement that moves us toward personal freedom. When we authentically love someone, our primary intent is to set them free. Father's forgiveness sets us free, giving us the internal capacity and desire to respond externally to God as a Father so we can hear His voice. To give us this freedom, Christ came to take us to the Father. Cultivating our relationship with Christ prepares us to more perfectly understand the Father. On the Cross, at the moment of His death, Jesus offered His Own human spirit to God the Father. Of course, all that Christ experienced and everything that occurred was born and facilitated by the Person of the Holy Spirit in preparation for this Eternal Lamb to be made a sin-offering, but He also gave up His Own human spirit. Christ has not only demonstrated His love for us, He has made intricate arrangements to participate with us, be present with us, and be our source of strength on our personal journey into God. In this Plumbline, Bob helps us get beyond our present application that Jesus' sacrifice was limited to our forgiveness. He gave Himself to us in every possible way—even in the complexities and crazies that life presents for the working out of our salvation. He gives Himself for us as the sacrificial Lamb of God. And, He gives His human spirit to us in order to conform us into the image of Himself.

ISBN 978-1-940054-09-4

LIFECHANGERS®

P.O. Box 3709 ❖ Cookeville, TN 38502
931.520.3730 ❖ lc@lifechangers.org

www.ingramcontent.com/pod-product-compliance
Lightning Source LLC
Chambersburg PA
CBHW071839020426
42331CB00007B/1791